Lucky 13
Survival in Space

Lucky 13
Survival in Space

Richard
Hilliard

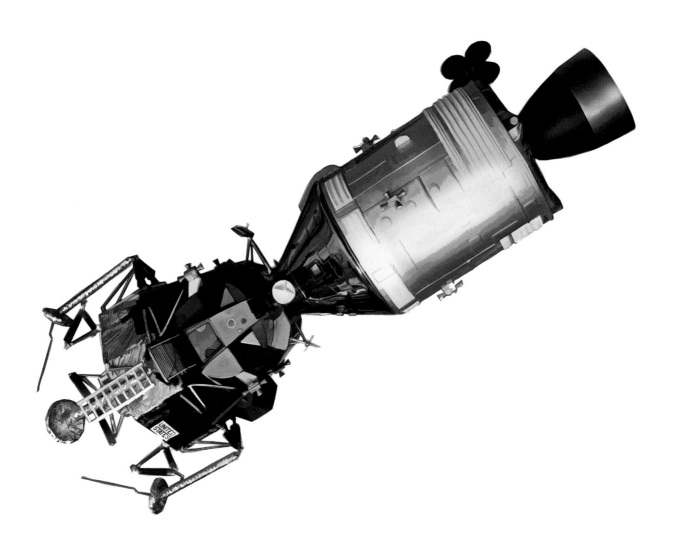

BOYDS MILLS PRESS

HONESDALE, PENNSYLVANIA

JUST LIKE MANY BOYS GROWING UP in the late 1930s, Jim Lovell read fantastic stories of space travel published in adventure magazines. He could not have imagined that one day he would be in a battle for survival far away from the planet Earth.

Jim grew up to be a U.S. Navy pilot and was chosen to become an astronaut in 1962, just as America was entering the "space age." This was a time of incredible achievements in space technology. On December 24, 1968, Jim was one of the first three astronauts to orbit the Moon in *Apollo 8*. Only seven months later, men from the Apollo 11 mission would walk on the Moon for the first time.

Apollo was the name given to the series of NASA missions that ultimately put humans on the Moon. The first missions involved testing the new Saturn V rocket and equipment in Earth's orbit, while later missions flew to the Moon, landed and explored its terrain, and brought the three astronauts back to Earth. *Apollo 8* was the first human mission to the Moon. It orbited Earth's closest neighbor in space but without landing on its surface. The historic landing occurred on July 20, 1969, with *Apollo 11*. Each subsequent mission lasted longer than the one before it, with the astronauts exploring different regions of the Moon and bringing back rock and soil samples for later study on Earth. From 1967 to 1972, the nine Apollo missions to the Moon proved that humans could explore other worlds.

JIM LOVELL
Born March 25, 1928,
in Cleveland, Ohio.
EDUCATION: University of Wisconsin;
bachelor of science degree from
the United States Naval Academy;
Naval Air Test Center (NATC) Test
Pilot School; University of Southern
California Aviation Safety School;
certificate, Advanced Management
Program, Harvard Business School.

FRED HAISE
Born November 14, 1933,
in Biloxi, Mississippi.
EDUCATION: Bachelor of science
degree with honors in aeronautical
engineering from the University of
Oklahoma.

JACK SWIGERT
Born August 30, 1931,
in Denver, Colorado.
EDUCATION: Bachelor of science degree
in mechanical engineering from the
University of Colorado; master of
science degree in aerospace science
from Rensselaer Polytechnic Institute;
master of business administration
degree from the University of Hartford.

Note: Jack Swigert was not the
original Command Module pilot of
Apollo 13. Just a few days before the
launch, he replaced astronaut Ken
Mattingly, who had been exposed to
measles. NASA decided it was too
much of a risk to allow Mattingly to
go into space.

After the historic success of Apollo 11 and Apollo 12, NASA selected
Jim Lovell, Fred Haise, and Jack Swigert as the crew of *Apollo 13*.
They were to be the third group of astronauts to land on the Moon.
Jim and Fred would explore the Moon's surface while Jack would
monitor the mission from lunar orbit.
Even though 13 was considered an
unlucky number, all
three astronauts felt
fortunate to be part
of the mission.

On April 11, 1970, Jim, Fred, and Jack were strapped into the command module sitting atop a mighty Saturn V rocket. They waited as the clock counted down to liftoff. When it reached zero, five giant rocket engines roared to life, carrying the three men away from Earth. The astronauts' families and people from miles around the Florida launch site watched as the three men sped toward the Moon!

The largest rocket ever successfully launched, the Saturn V was a giant even by current standards. Standing 363 feet tall, it held almost five million pounds of highly explosive rocket fuel, most of which was needed to escape Earth's gravity and put the crew into space. Because of the rocket's power, people who came to the launch site to witness the liftoff were kept at least three miles away in case an accident occured. If a Saturn V rocket had malfunctioned during liftoff, the explosion would have been comparable to a small atomic bomb. However, there were never any significant problems with the Saturn V, and it proved to be one of the safest rockets ever built, carrying nine Apollo missions to the Moon.

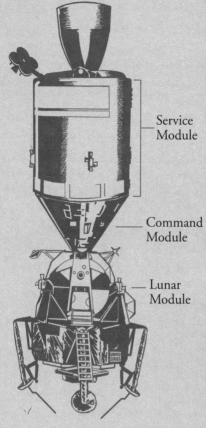

Service
Module

Command
Module

Lunar
Module

Once the rocket booster engines
were used and discarded, only
the Command, Service, and
Lunar Modules were needed
to get the crew to the Moon
and back home again. The
Command Module, named
Odyssey, was the primary living
and working quarters for the
three astronauts during their
journey, while the Lunar
Module, named *Aquarius*,
would be used only to take two
of the crew members down
to the lunar surface. During
the landing and exploration
of the Moon, one of the team
would remain in the Command
Module that stayed in lunar
orbit, monitoring the Lunar
Module and its crew. After
the astronauts explored the
Moon, the top half of the Lunar
Module would rocket back into
lunar orbit, leaving the bottom
half on the lunar surface, and
rejoin the Command Module,
reuniting the three astronauts.
The Lunar Module would
then be discarded, and the
Command and Service Modules
would return to Earth.

As the rocket stages containing empty fuel tanks were discarded, the Command and Service Modules turned around in space and latched onto the Lunar Module, which would carry Jim and Fred to the Moon's surface. Jack carefully piloted the Command Module during this critical docking maneuver. All systems were "go" for landing on the Moon.

Houston's Mission Control was a massive facility dedicated to keeping track of the Apollo mission's status before, during, and after the launch. In charge was the flight director, who made critical mission decisions along with the crew. Based on information given to him by the Apollo crew and his team of ground-based technicians, the flight director would decide whether the mission would continue along the established flight plan. The alternative was to "abort," which means abandoning the main plan and going to a backup in case of an emergency. During a mission, three flight directors would alternate at eight-hour intervals. The flight directors for Apollo 13 were Gerald Griffin, Gene Krantz, and Glen Lunney.

Krantz

Lunney

Griffin

Back on Earth, the technicians at Mission Control in Houston, Texas, watched closely. Their monitors and communications with the crew of *Apollo 13* showed everything going smoothly. After the successful docking, the flight director ordered the crew to carry out some routine procedures that would prepare for the Moon landing. The date was April 13.

Suddenly, outside the Command Module was a violent explosion! Precious oxygen was pouring out the side of the Service Module, and the spacecraft began to lose power as well. Within minutes, Jim knew that he and Fred would not be able to walk on the Moon. As the situation became clear to the men, they realized that unless they worked fast, they might not make it back to Earth safely. Jim told Mission Control, "Houston, we have a problem."

As soon as Mission Control fully understood the situation, the team quickly focused on how to get the men back to Earth in the badly crippled spacecraft. One of the primary oxygen tanks in the Service Module had exploded because of a defective electrical switch. And they realized that the explosion had damaged the batteries powering the Command Module as well as the oxygen supply

needed for fuel and life support. Mission Control determined the only thing that could keep the crew alive was to use the Lunar Module as a lifeboat and modify its systems to support the three men struggling to survive in the cold vacuum of space.

During the entire journey, data on every part of the mission was radioed back to Mission Control to monitor. From the crew's heartbeats and respiration to the smallest workings of the spacecraft, Mission Control kept watch. As data poured in after the explosion, the team in Houston determined that the landing mission now became one of simple survival. The Command and Service Modules would barely have enough power to get the crew through reentry into Earth's atmosphere, so the Lunar Module would have to be used to get them the nearly two hundred thousand miles back home. With the Command and Service Modules dead in space, the small cabin of the Lunar Module would have to sustain the astronauts on the long, lonely journey back to Earth.

Jack Swigert was one of the few unmarried astronauts at NASA during the Apollo program, but both Jim Lovell and Fred Haise had large families back on Earth, families that were living in fear once the accident had become known to them. Jim and Marilyn had four children, while Fred and Patt Haise had three, with a fourth child on the way. Watching the television and waiting for the regular updates from Mission Control, they knew how dangerous the situation was but were helpless to do anything about it. Adding to the stress of the ordeal, the families' homes were surrounded by members of the media once the story broke out. Suddenly, what was once considered a "routine" mission became front-page news. With the world watching in anticipation, the crew's wives and children were caught in the middle.

Mission Control and the crew of *Apollo 13* were not the only ones dealing with the deadly problem. Back at home, their families tried to cope with the reality that the men might not make it back. Jim's wife, Marilyn, stayed in constant contact with Houston and hoped that, against all odds, her husband would return to her and their children. Whatever the outcome, she and the other family members knew that the NASA team was doing everything possible to bring the crew back safely.

The badly damaged ship orbited once around the Moon, using the Moon's gravity to turn toward Earth without using up precious fuel. From the window of the Lunar Module, Jim looked at the Moon. He knew that he would never walk on its surface. They were still a long way from home, and nothing was certain.

As time slowly passed, more problems became apparent inside the Lunar Module lifeboat. The three-day journey began to feel like a lifetime. Jack had to modify one of the air filters from the Command Module because the oxygen levels were dropping dangerously low, and Fred showed signs of a fever from a minor infection. Because the computer had to be shut down, Jim worked with pencil and paper to make the scientific calculations that would bring them home. With Earth getting closer and closer, the men had to prepare to reenter Earth's atmosphere.

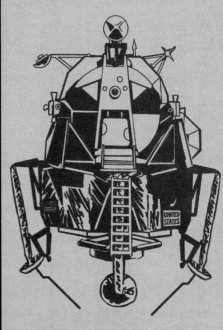

The Lunar Module was designed with one purpose: land two astronauts on the Moon, allow them to exit the vehicle, and, after reentering, transport them and collected soil samples back to the Command Module. The spacecraft was built with the lightest materials possible and was not as sturdy as the Command Module. Parts of the Lunar Module's outer skin were only as thick as three pieces of aluminum foil. It took a lot of work to make it capable of supporting three astronauts as a "lifeboat." The air filtration systems had to be modified using materials held together with hoses and duct tape, and the heating system could not be used in order to conserve power. The cold, cramped Lunar Module was the crew's only chance to survive.

As the crippled ship moved closer to Earth, the crew returned to the Command Module, because the Lunar Module was not equipped to reenter Earth's atmosphere. Using energy from the Lunar Module, they had to "power up" the ship in a very precise way, or the batteries would fail. Once this was accomplished, the Lunar Module and Service Module were discarded, and the crew could see the damage caused by the explosion for the first time. Almost the entire side of the Service Module had been destroyed by the force of the blast, and though they were now close to home, other possible problems arose. If the explosion had damaged the heat shield on the bottom of the Command Module, the intense heat generated by reentry would consume the spacecraft and the crew with it. With time running out, all they could do was trust their training and hope for a little luck.

Going back into the Command Module, the three men brought the ship back to life, one step at a time. Separating from the Service Module and later the Lunar Module, the Command Module began the fiery descent back to Earth. If their calculations were incorrect, they could possibly skip off the atmosphere or burn up upon reentry. Also, if the explosion had damaged the module's heat shield, they would not make it back even if their calculations were right. Millions of people all over the world held their breath as the three men hurtled through the atmosphere.

During reentry, communication with the spacecraft was impossible, and the minutes silently ticked by. The tension felt by everyone at Mission Control suddenly erupted into thunderous cheers and applause as the spacecraft appeared on the big video screen, the module's three giant parachutes safely lowering it to the gentle waves of the Pacific Ocean.

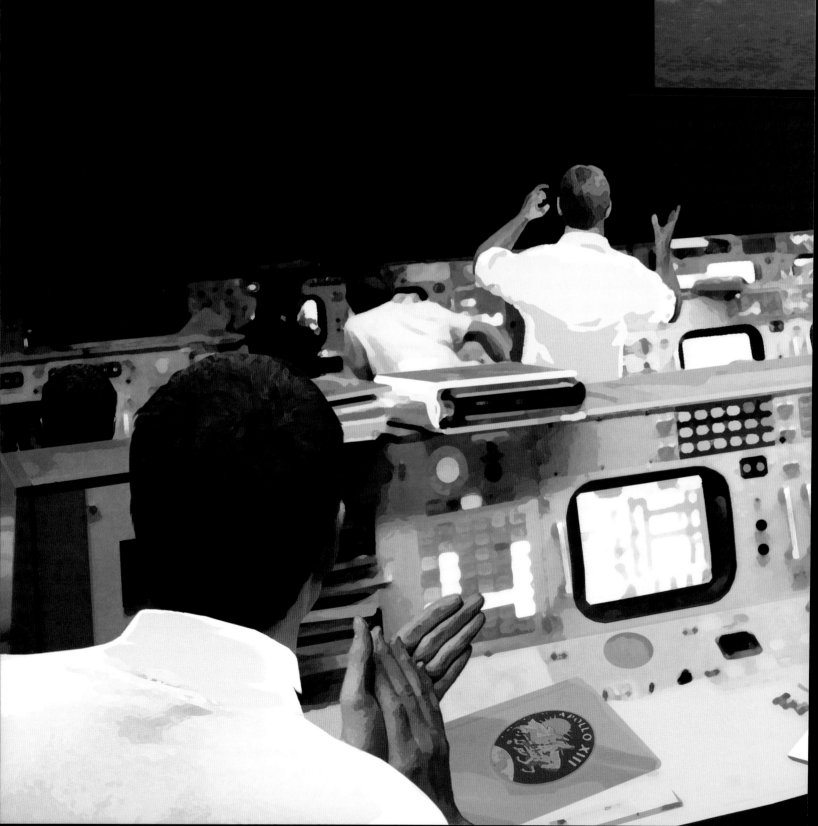

As the crew fell through Earth's atmosphere at speeds capable of turning the spacecraft into a fireball, their only protection was the heat shield. At the height of the Command Module's fiery reentry, communication with Mission Control was impossible because of the rushing energy surrounding the capsule. This blackout could last for minutes, and no one on the ground would know if the astronauts were safe. After an agonizing four-minute blackout, the crew of *Apollo 13* radioed back to Mission Control that the three huge parachutes had deployed for splashdown and that the men were safely descending to the Pacific. The astronauts were picked up by waiting helicopters as everyone breathed a sigh of relief. Although the crew of *Apollo 13* did not land on the Moon, their successful return to Earth was a cause for celebration around the world.

Back on Earth, Jim, Fred, and Jack were welcomed as heroes and reunited with their families. The ordeal of *Apollo 13* proved that teamwork could overcome nearly impossible odds and that humankind's exploration of space would continue despite the dangers that would surely lie ahead.

U.S.S. IWO JIMA
ASTRONAUT
SWIGERT
APOLLO13
U.S.S. IWO JIMA
ASTRONAUT
HAISE
APOLLO13
NASA
NASA
APOLLO XIII

For Kenneth and Yvonne Hilliard, Barbara Halifko,
and Charlotte Long—supportive parents all

Special thanks to
my wife, Adrienne; Vincent Di Fate; Ted and Betsy Lewin;
Murray Tinkelman; Joyce Burns; Bill Thomson; and Roger D. Launius, Ph.D., chair,
Division of Space History, Smithsonian National Air and Space Museum

Text and illustrations copyright © 2008 by Richard Hilliard

Boyds Mills Press, Inc.
815 Church Street
Honesdale, Pennsylvania 18431
Printed in China

Library of Congress Cataloging-in-Publication Data

Hilliard, Richard.
Lucky 13 : survival in space / Richard Hilliard. — 1st ed.
p. cm.
ISBN 978-1-59078-557-7 (hardcover : alk. paper)
1. Apollo 13 (Spacecraft) 2. Project Apollo (U.S.) 3. Space vehicle accidents. I. Title. II. Title: Lucky thirteen.
TL789.8.U6A535256 2008
629.45'4—dc22
2007051237

First edition
The text of this book is set in 12-point Garamond.
The illustrations are done in acrylic.
10 9 8 7 6 5 4 3 2 1